SPOTLIGHT on Adjustment Disorder in Adolescents

Recognizing Signs and Providing Support

Gerald M. Trexler

Table of Content

Adolescence, a key era defined by physical, emotional, and social upheavals, is naturally a period of transition. For some teens, managing these changes becomes a daunting task, leading to adjustment disorder—a frequently ignored mental health condition that requires our close attention. In this research, we focus on Adjustment Disorder in Adolescents, hoping to get a better understanding of the specific obstacles that young people with this disease confront.

Uncovering Unique Challenges:

Adolescents with adjustment disorder have unique challenges that are tightly woven into the fabric of their developmental path. The influence of puberty, hormonal variations, scholastic stress, and rising social expectations produce a fragile environment in which emotional well-being might be threatened. This investigation aims to offer insight into the particular issues that teenagers face, including the junction of biological changes, social pressures, and mental health.

Recognizing early signs:
Recognizing early indications and symptoms of adjustment disorder in teenagers is critical to treating it. Critical signs include behavioral alterations, emotional instability, and interruptions in academic and social settings. Understanding these warning indicators enables parents, educators, and caregivers to distinguish between typical adolescent swings and chronic symptoms that need assistance.

Guidelines for Support:
This initiative is more than just an analysis of issues; it is also a practical guidance for individuals who care about the well-being of teenagers. Parents, educators, and caregivers play critical responsibilities in identifying and providing appropriate assistance. Our investigation is built on strategies for open communication, collaborative methods, and resilience development. Through this entire journey, we want to provide people with the skills and insights they need to negotiate the difficulties of adolescent adjustment disorder, while also cultivating a culture of understanding, compassion, and proactive support.

Chapter 1: Adolescent Adjustment Disorder Overview

Adolescence, a dynamic stage distinguished by self-discovery and fast growth, is essentially a period of adjustment. However, for certain teenagers, the process of adjusting to big life changes may be very difficult, resulting in the development of adjustment disorder. This mental health illness is defined by emotional and behavioral abnormalities that occur in reaction to certain stresses or life events.

Diagnostic Characteristics:

Adolescent adjustment disorder is recognized using a specific set of criteria. The Diagnostic and Statistical Manual of Mental Disorders (DSM-5) highlights critical characteristics, stressing that symptoms must appear within three months after the initiation of a stressor and be disproportionate events abnormal in nature. The stressor might be a significant life event like parental divorce, relocation, scholastic challenges, or interpersonal disputes.

Common Presentations:

Adolescent adjustment disorder manifests itself in a variety of ways, including emotional, behavioral, and social shifts. Emotional symptoms may include excessive concern, despair, or hopelessness. Behavioral indicators may include retreat from typical activities, changes in academic achievement, or changes in interpersonal interactions.

Differentiation from typical adolescent challenges:

Identifying adjustment disorder requires distinguishing between typical developmental hurdles and chronic maladaptive reactions. Adolescents often deal with mood fluctuations, identity discovery, and scholastic stress. However, adjustment disorder causes a significant disturbance in everyday functioning, much above the usual oscillations associated with adolescence.

Risk factors and vulnerabilities:

Certain variables, such as a history of trauma, pre-existing mental health issues, or restricted support networks, may raise an adolescent's risk of developing adjustment disorder. Understanding the risk factors is critical for early detection and management.

Impact on daily life:

Adjustment disorder may have a substantial influence on many elements of an adolescent's life, including academic success, social interactions, and general health. Recognizing the possible long-term implications emphasizes the significance of immediate intervention and assistance.

Holistic Approach to Treatment:

Addressing adjustment disorder in teenagers requires a comprehensive strategy that takes into account the complexities of their lives. Collaboration among mental health experts, parents, educators, and caregivers is critical for fostering a supportive atmosphere favorable to healing and rehabilitation.

The importance of recognizing and addressing the issue

Escalation Prevention: Early detection of adjustment problems enables early management, preventing emotional and behavioral issues from escalating. By recognizing the signs and symptoms, parents, educators, and caregivers may provide an atmosphere favorable to treating stresses before they worsen.

Enhanced Academic Performance: Adjustment disorder may have a significant influence on academic functioning, resulting in decreased performance and interest. Recognizing the problem allows educational professionals to provide tailored support techniques, creating an environment in which teenagers may succeed academically despite the obstacles they may face.

Improved Interpersonal interactions: Adolescents with adjustment disorder often experience disturbances in interpersonal interactions, both within the family and among peers. Recognizing these problems allows parents and caregivers to establish open communication, resulting in a supportive network that promotes the adolescent's emotional well-being.

Reduced Stigma Surrounding Mental Health: Addressing adjustment disorder fosters an environment of openness and acceptance around mental health. By addressing and discussing mental health problems, we assist to reduce the stigma associated with getting treatment and create an atmosphere in which teenagers feel comfortable sharing their challenges.

Optimal Developmental Outcomes: Adolescence is an important stage in cognitive, emotional, and social development. Recognizing and intervening in adjustment disorder leads to better developmental outcomes, ensuring that adolescents handle obstacles in ways that enhance resilience, coping skills, and long-term well-being.

Family and Community help: Understanding adjustment disorder enables families and communities to provide focused help. Recognizing the influence of stresses and disturbances on an adolescent's mental health allows for a collaborative approach in which parents, educators, and community members work together to provide a nurturing environment.

Long-Term Mental Health Resilience: Treating adjustment disorder establishes the groundwork for long-term mental health resilience. By offering timely assistance and tools, we help adolescents build coping strategies, emotional regulation skills, and self-efficacy that will serve them long into adulthood.

In summary, diagnosing and treating adjustment disorder in teenagers entails not just addressing current issues, but also creating an environment that fosters healthy growth, resilience, and a good attitude toward mental health. It is a common obligation that, when performed, benefits both teenagers and the communities to which they belong.

Chapter 2: Understanding Adjustment Disorder in Adolescents

Definition and Diagnostic Criteria

Adjustment Disorder in Adolescents is a psychological illness marked by the emergence of emotional or behavioral symptoms in response to certain stresses. These stresses might include big life events or continuing issues, causing severe impairment in everyday functioning.

Diagnostic criteria:

- Emotional or behavioral signs appear within three months after a stressor's initiation.
- The symptoms go beyond what is normally anticipated in reaction to the stressor.
- The symptoms lead to clinically substantial discomfort or impairment in social, academic, or other aspects of functioning.
- The symptoms are not entirely caused by another mental illness.

Spotlight on Adjustment Disorder in Adolescents helps you recognize indications including mood swings, scholastic deterioration, and changes in social behavior. It highlights the need for early detection and provides recommendations on how to provide vital assistance to teenagers dealing with difficult life situations.

Differentiating from normal adolescent development.

Distinguishing Adjustment Disorder from normal teenage growth is critical for successful identification and assistance. While teenagers often experience mood swings and identity exploration, several symptoms of Adjustment Disorder stand out:

Intensity and Duration: Adjustment Disorder symptoms are more severe and prolonged than ordinary teenage mood fluctuations. The anguish and impairment should be out of proportion to the stressor and linger for longer than anticipated.

Impaired Functioning: Watch for major disruptions in everyday functioning, such as poor academic achievement, troubled relationships, or retreat from formerly enjoyable hobbies. These disturbances go beyond the transient difficulties associated with adolescence.

Identifiable Stressor: Adjustment disorder necessitates a clear link between symptoms and a particular stressor. Understanding the source and effect of the stressor is critical for separating it from typical developmental problems.

Unresponsiveness to Supportive Interventions: If an adolescent's problems continue despite help from family, friends, or school, it might be a sign of adjustment disorder. Normal growth often entails overcoming obstacles with external aid.

Chapter 3: Adolescent Challenges, including the impact of puberty and hormonal changes.

Puberty and hormonal changes have a profound influence on comprehending the specific issues that adolescents experience, especially those associated with Adjustment Disorder.

Emotional Turmoil: Puberty causes hormonal swings, which may exacerbate emotional experiences. Adolescents may experience mood fluctuations, increased sensitivity, and susceptibility to stresses, which might contribute to the development of Adjustment Disorder symptoms.

Identity development: Hormonal changes coincide with a critical period of identity development. Adolescents may struggle with self-discovery, body image issues, and cultural expectations, which exacerbate the difficulties they endure. Adjustment When these problems outweigh their coping skills, a disorder may develop.

Social Dynamics: Hormonal changes may influence interpersonal interactions. Adolescents may have difficulties in creating and sustaining relationships, leading to feelings of loneliness. Recognizing the influence of these hormone shifts is critical to understanding the social context of Adjustment Disorder.

Academic Pressure and Social Expectations

Academic demands and social expectations provide considerable obstacles for teenagers, adding to the complications discussed in the Spotlight on Adjustment Disorder in teenagers.

Scholastic Pressures: Adolescents often face higher scholastic pressures, such as tests, assignments, and future professional plans. These demands may cause stress, worry, and feelings of inadequacy, which may contribute to Adjustment Disorder symptoms including academic deterioration, disengagement, or avoidance.

Adolescents negotiate a complicated social terrain that includes demands from peers, family, and society. Trying to fit in, satisfy society's standards, or adapt to peer norms may cause stress. Adjustment Disorder may develop when an adolescent's capacity to adjust is overwhelmed by societal demands.

Peer Relationships: Social dynamics, peer pressure, and the need for acceptability may all cause stress in teenagers. Challenges in developing and sustaining friendships, along with a fear of social judgment, may lead to Adjustment Disorder symptoms relating to social functioning.

Chapter 4: Early Signs and Symptoms

Behavioral Indicators

As described in Spotlight on Adjustment Disorder in Teenagers: spotting Signs and Providing Support, behavioral indications are critical for spotting signs of the disorder in teenagers. These signs include observable activities that differ from an adolescent's usual behavior, indicating probable psychological discomfort. Here are extensive descriptions of several important behavioral indicators:

Withdrawal: Adolescents with Adjustment Disorder may withdraw from social activities, distancing themselves from friends, family, and formerly valued hobbies. This retreat might show as spending more time alone or avoiding social contact.

Changes in Academic Performance: Academic performance declines, such as a rapid reduction in grades or a loss of interest in school-related activities, may indicate Adjustment Disorder. These alterations may reflect the effects of pressures on the adolescent's capacity to focus and learn.

Irritability and Agitation: Behavioral changes toward irritability, rage, or heightened agitation may be seen. These feelings may be displayed in reaction to pressures that are beyond the adolescent's coping ability, showing the internal turmoil associated with Adjustment Disorder.

Risk-Taking activities: Some teenagers may engage in hazardous activities to deal with pressures. This may involve drug misuse, irresponsible driving, or participating in potentially dangerous activities. These activities may be maladaptive efforts to cope with overwhelming emotions.

Disruptions in sleep and eating patterns, such as insomnia or increased/decreased hunger, may be visible. These alterations might indicate the physiological influence of stress on the adolescent's general well-being.

Physical Complaints: Adolescents with Adjustment Disorder may have physical symptoms such as headaches, stomachaches, and exhaustion. These somatic problems may not have an underlying medical reason but rather are related to the disorder's psychological suffering.

Emotional Warning Signs

As mentioned in Spotlight on Adjustment Disorder in Adolescents, emotional warning indicators play an important role in detecting the disorder. Recognizing Signs and Providing Assistance. These indications include visible changes in an adolescent's emotional well-being that suggest the existence of mental discomfort. The following are thorough descriptions of emotional warning flags related to Adjustment Disorder:

Adolescents with Adjustment Disorder may have continuous emotions of severe despair or hopelessness that go beyond the typical emotional changes of adolescence. This emotional state might be disproportionate to the specified stressor.

Excessive Worry or Anxiety: A high degree of worry or anxiety, even in the face of small stresses, may indicate Adjustment Disorder. This emotional response might emerge as excessive worry about the future, academic achievement, or social relationships.

Irritability and wrath: Excessive irritability, mood swings, or unusual outbursts of wrath may indicate emotional discomfort. These feelings might be the result of an inability to deal successfully with stress, which causes increased emotional reactivity.

Emotions of Guilt or Shame: Adolescents suffering from Adjustment Disorder may have inappropriate emotions of guilt or shame, which are often tied to their perceived incapacity to cope with stress or satisfy expectations. These emotional reactions might lead to feelings of self-blame.

Loss of Interest or Pleasure: A significant reduction in interest or pleasure in formerly pleasurable activities may be seen. Adolescents may retreat from hobbies, social connections, or extracurricular activities as a result of an overwhelming sensation of emotional disengagement.

Low self-esteem: adjustment. The disorder may be related to a drop in self-esteem. Adolescents may have poor self-perceptions, feeling inadequate or undeserving in the face of pressures and hardships.

Emotional Expression Changes: Emotional expression changes, such as a flat affect or a lack of reaction to pleasant stimuli, may be signs of emotional distress. Adolescents may struggle to articulate and feel a wide variety of emotions.

Academic and Social Changes

Academic and social changes are crucial indicators of Adjustment Disorder in teenagers, providing vital insights into their psychological well-being. In the context of Spotlight on Adjustment Disorder in Adolescents: Recognizing Signs and Providing Support, these changes include both academic and social changes. Here's a full analysis of these indicators:

Academic Changes:

Academic Performance Decline: A significant loss in grades, a change in study habits, or an abrupt drop in academic involvement may indicate Adjustment Disorder. Academic difficulties may worsen as the teenager attempts to deal with pressure.

Adolescents suffering from Adjustment Disorder may engage in avoidance activities linked to academic duties. This might involve skipping classes, delaying tasks, or putting off previously achievable obligations.

Decreased Motivation: A considerable drop in motivation and interest in learning may occur. Adolescents may experience sentiments of indifference or lack of passion for academic activities, indicating the influence of psychological discomfort on academic participation.

Changes in Attendance: Frequent absence or a drop in school attendance may indicate Adjustment Disorder. Adolescent pressures may lead to a lack of willingness or capacity to engage in the school environment.

Social Changes:
Isolation or Social Withdrawal: Adolescents with Adjustment Disorder may withdraw from social activities. This retreat might show as more time

spent alone, avoiding social gatherings, or a reluctance to interact with peers and relatives.

Conflict in Relationships: The influence of pressures on an adolescent's mental condition may result in greater conflict in relationships. As the teenager deals with the difficulties of Adjustment Disorder, his or her connections with friends, family, or classmates may become increasingly strained.

Loss of Interest in Social Activities: You may notice a decrease in your interest or engagement in social activities, extracurriculars, or hobbies. Adolescents may disengage from previously appreciated social activities owing to the emotional cost of pressures.

Peer Rejection or Isolation: Social difficulties may extend to peer interactions, causing rejection or isolation from social groups. Adolescents with Adjustment Disorder may have difficulty connecting with others, worsening feelings of loneliness and social isolation.

Chapter 5: Recognizing Adjustment Disorder vs. Typical Teen Behavior

Differentiating Normal Adolescent Mood Swings.

Mood swings are a normal feature of adolescent behavior. However, differentiating between natural oscillations and Adjustment Disorder (AD) requires assessing the duration and severity of symptoms. Normal mood swings are usually transient and caused by hormonal fluctuations, but AD is characterized by more protracted and disruptive emotional responses to stresses.

Recognizing indicators of Alzheimer's disease involves monitoring persistent sensations of melancholy, worry, or irritation that go beyond what is considered normal. In addition, decreased social or academic performance, as well as behavioral changes such as withdrawal or recklessness, may suggest Adjustment Disorder.

Providing support entails encouraging open conversation with teenagers, understanding their feelings, and assisting them in dealing with challenges. If symptoms continue or seriously affect everyday living, professional involvement, such as counseling or therapy, may be required for an accurate evaluation and treatment.

Identifying persistent or escalating symptoms

Identifying persistent or worsening symptoms is critical in separating Adjustment Disorder (AD) from usual adolescent behavior. While some mood fluctuations are natural, chronic and intense emotional responses to stimuli may indicate Alzheimer's disease.

Mood swings are common in adolescence and are usually short-lived and controllable. However, with Alzheimer's disease, symptoms last for a long time and might worsen, affecting many parts of the adolescent's life.

A protracted period of symptoms, such as persistent melancholy, anxiety, or behavioral abnormalities, becomes an important component. Furthermore, an increase in the intensity or frequency of emotional responses above what is expected for adolescents signals a need for more attention and maybe professional help.

Early detection of persistent or worsening symptoms enables immediate intervention and support, which is critical for successfully treating Adjustment Disorder in adolescents.

Chapter 6: The Parent's Role in Recognition and Support

Building Open Communication

Open communication between parents and teenagers is essential for detecting indicators of Adjustment Disorder (AD) and offering appropriate assistance. Parents play an important role in providing an atmosphere in which teenagers feel comfortable expressing their feelings. Here are the detailed steps.

- Establish trust by creating a non-judgmental environment that acknowledges and respects the adolescent's sentiments

- Active listening involves paying complete attention, maintaining eye contact, and validating the feelings stated by the teenager.

- Encourage uninhibited expression of ideas and emotions. Allow the teenager to relate their experiences without fear of condemnation.

- Open-ended inquiries may foster discourse and provide deeper insights into an adolescent's emotional condition. Avoid yes/no questions to elicit more detailed replies.

Normalize Emotions: Adolescents may feel many emotions at this developmental time. Recognize that mood fluctuations are normal, but underline the need to communicate persistent or severe emotions.

Be Patient and Empathetic: Recognize that teenagers may struggle to express their feelings. Validate their feelings and emotions while demonstrating empathy.

Educate Adolescents about Adjustment Disorder: Treat them to realize that getting treatment is a proactive step towards improving their mental health.

Collaborative problem-solving involves adolescents in identifying answers to pressures and obstacles. This promotes a feeling of autonomy and empowerment.

Provide Supportive services: Educate yourself on available mental health services and be ready to refer the teenager to professional care if necessary.

Establishing frequent check-ins might help establish an ongoing discussion about emotions and well-being. Consistency in communicating increases feelings of security.

Active participation in open communication allows parents to better notice early indicators of Adjustment Disorder, give timely assistance, and contribute to their teenagers' overall mental health and well-being.

Strategies to Create a Supportive Environment

Creating a supportive atmosphere is critical for parents in detecting the indicators of Adjustment Disorder (AD) and giving adequate assistance to teenagers. Here are comprehensive techniques for creating such an environment:

Create an emotionally safe environment where teenagers may express their emotions without fear of judgment. This promotes transparency and honesty.

Establish open communication by actively listening, asking open-ended questions, and being accessible. Make sure that teenagers are comfortable communicating their issues and feelings.

Build trust via empathy and understanding. Recognize the difficulties of youth, normalize emotions, and emphasize your support.

Respect Individual Differences: Value each adolescent's unique identity. Recognize that their experiences and emotions may vary, and avoid making assumptions.

Establish a consistent pattern, including regular family time and check-ins. Consistency offers stability, and periodic check-ins enable continuous talks about well-being.

Encourage independence by engaging teenagers in decision-making processes. Empower them to accept responsibility for their choices and behaviors.

Model appropriate coping techniques to manage stress and obstacles. Parents act as role models, and demonstrating healthy emotional management techniques helps to foster a supportive atmosphere.

Encourage healthy lifestyle choices, such as getting enough sleep, eating well, and exercising often. Physical well-being is intimately related to mental health.

Establish clear and fair limits to provide structure. Adolescents feel safer and more predictable when there are consistent limits in place.

Seek expert help: Proactively seek expert help as required. Familiarize yourself with relevant mental health services and work with specialists to guarantee thorough care.

Acknowledge and appreciate successes, great or little. Positive reinforcement promotes a helpful and encouraging atmosphere.

Demonstrate unconditional love and acceptance. Adolescents must understand that their parents will always be there for them, no matter what obstacles or failures they face.

By applying these methods, parents may provide a supportive atmosphere that promotes mental health, aids in the early detection of Adjustment Disorder, and allows for effective care when necessary.

Recognizing Signs in Classrooms

Recognizing indications of Adjustment Disorder (AD) in the classroom allows educators to give timely help to teenagers. Here are some techniques from an educator's perspective:

Actively monitor and document pupils' behavior, attitude, and interactions. Keep careful records of any changes in academic achievement, social contacts, or general temperament.

Understanding normal teenage behavior might help identify variations that may signal Alzheimer's disease. Understand that although some mood swings are natural, persistent or excessive fluctuations may raise worry.

Establish open contact with peers to identify behavioral or emotional changes. Peers often notice changes that instructors may overlook.

Conduct frequent check-ins with students to foster a friendly and accessible environment. Encourage kids to express their views and emotions, so building trust.

Maintain open contact with parents to address any issues or changes noted in the classroom. A collaborative approach provides a thorough grasp of the adolescent's well-being.

Monitor academic achievement and note any declines or changes in motivation. Adjustment Disorders might impair a student's capacity to focus and study.

Identify Social retreat or hostility: Observe changes in social conduct, such as retreat from peers or increasing hostility. These fluctuations might be suggestive of emotional difficulties associated with Adjustment Disorder.

Refer to school counselors or mental health professionals.

If the symptoms continue or worsen, see school counselors or mental health specialists. They may perform further evaluations and provide relevant assistance or recommendations for action.

Foster a secure and inclusive classroom climate where students may freely express their feelings. This may aid in the early detection of any adjustment issues.

Promote peer support by creating a supportive atmosphere where students watch out for one another. This may aid in spotting indicators of distress and providing timely care when necessary.

Offer flexible learning options, knowing that certain students may need adjustments during hard times. This may reduce further stress.

Stay educated about mental health options available in your school or community. Knowing about support systems provides for prompt help when needed.

Educators who actively use these tactics may play a critical role in spotting indicators of Adjustment Disorder in the classroom and ensuring that adolescents get the emotional care they need.

Collaborative approaches with parents

Collaborative methods with parents are critical for educators in detecting and supporting teenagers, particularly in recognizing indicators of Adjustment Disorder (AD). Here's a thorough look at such joint strategies:

Establish open, transparent communication channels with parents. Regular reports on academic achievement, conduct, and any concerns help to build a common picture of the adolescent's well-being.

Conduct frequent parent-teacher conferences to review students' academic and socio-emotional growth. This allows the sharing of observations and ideas.

Promptly report any observations or concerns about the adolescent's behavior, mood, or academic achievement. Collaborative problem-solving works better when both instructors and parents are informed of the issue.

Provide resources and information about Adjustment Disorder, including indications and symptoms. This teaches parents and prepares them to identify possible symptoms at home.

Encourage parents to examine their child's behavior at home, including changes in mood, sleep habits, and social contacts. This comprehensive approach benefits early detection.

Collaborate on solutions for assistance, both at school and at home. This may include making changes to the learning environment, establishing coping methods, or seeking external professional help.

Involve school counselors in cooperation. Counselors may give extra insights and assistance by serving as liaisons between educators and parents in dealing with adjustment issues.

Create joint intervention strategies as required. This might include tailored academic techniques, counseling sessions, or the engagement of mental health specialists, including feedback from both educators and parents.

Establish regular communication mechanisms to keep instructors and parents aware of progress on time. This creates a feeling of shared responsibility for the adolescent's well-being.

Respect cultural and familial dynamics while resolving adjustment challenges. Respect different points of view and ideals while working together.

Encourage parental involvement in their children's education and well-being. Involvement may go beyond academics to include emotional and social support.

Follow-up on suggestions: Regularly examine the efficacy of implemented suggestions and tactics. Adjust the assistance plan as required in response to continuous cooperation and feedback.

By building a collaborative collaboration with parents, educators may develop a comprehensive support structure that improves the diagnosis of Adjustment Disorder symptoms and assures a coordinated effort to help teenagers navigate these problems.

Chapter 8: Guidance for Caregivers: Navigating Treatment and Support

Seeking Professional Help

Seeking professional assistance for caregivers navigating therapy and support in the setting of adjustment disorder in teenagers entails detecting indicators and giving critical support. Caregivers should be aware of behavioral changes in teenagers, such as retreat, academic deterioration, or mood swings, which may indicate adjustment issues. Collaborating with mental health specialists, such as psychiatrists or therapists, is critical.

Starting the procedure is finding a certified mental health professional who specializes in teenage adjustment concerns. Establishing open contact with the healthcare professional helps to share insights and concerns. Professionals may perform evaluations to establish the degree and precise type of adjustment disorder, which will aid in the formulation of a personalized treatment strategy.

Psychotherapy, cognitive-behavioral therapy (CBT), and family therapy are common treatment approaches used to address underlying difficulties and enhance coping abilities. Medication may be used in extreme situations. Caregivers play an important role in facilitating the treatment process by reinforcing therapeutic practices at home and creating a supportive atmosphere.

Ongoing communication with specialists allows caregivers to assess progress and make necessary changes to the treatment plan. Furthermore, caregiver support groups and educational materials may offer helpful insights and coping skills for teenagers dealing with adjustment issues.

In summary, getting professional help entails detecting symptoms, selecting appropriate mental health specialists, communicating openly, participating in the treatment process, and obtaining further assistance via caregiver networks or educational resources.

Family-Centered Approaches to Recovery

Family-centered methods for rehabilitation in the setting of adolescent adjustment disorder highlight the family's important role in giving support and creating a positive environment for the teenager's well-being. These techniques understand that family relationships have a substantial influence on an adolescent's mental health and rehabilitation.

Assessment of Family Dynamics:
Professionals first examine family dynamics to determine any relevant elements or pressures inside the family. Understanding the family's structure, communication patterns, and connections helps design treatments to meet unique requirements.

Psychoeducation in Families:
Caregivers get psychoeducation about adjustment problems, their symptoms, and their influence on adolescents. This information enables families to identify symptoms, eliminate stigma, and actively engage in the rehabilitation process.

Communication Skill Training:
Caregivers develop good communication skills to foster open interaction with teenagers. Improved communication promotes understanding, aids in the identification of triggers, and strengthens the family's overall support system.

Family therapy sessions:
Family therapy consists of collaborative sessions with the teenager and caretakers. Therapists facilitate talks to address root causes, enhance family dynamics, and build relationships. Collaborative problem-solving becomes a focal point for overcoming obstacles together.

Establishing supportive routines:
Developing organized and supportive routines at home helps to ensure the stability of the adolescent's surroundings. Consistent routines, positive reinforcement, and clear expectations provide a feeling of stability and routine for adolescents.

Encourage Family Involvement in Treatment:
Family members actively engage in the treatment plan, which reinforces the therapeutic tactics outlined in individual therapy sessions. This

engagement facilitates the integration of coping methods and support structures into the adolescent's and family's everyday life.

Identifying and addressing family stressors:
Family-centered techniques include detecting and treating any external stresses influencing the family unit. Financial difficulties, academic concerns, and family disputes may all lead to an adjustment disorder.

Ongoing Collaboration with Professionals:
Continuous cooperation with mental health specialists guarantees that the family-centered approach is adaptable to the changing requirements of the adolescent and family. Regular check-ins allow you to track your progress and make modifications to your treatment plan as needed.

In conclusion, family-centered methods of adjustment disorder rehabilitation provide caregivers with information, communication skills, and active participation in the treatment process. These treatments, which address family dynamics and provide a supportive environment, make a substantial contribution to an adolescent's overall health and rehabilitation.

Chapter 9: Prevention and Resilience Building

Proactive Strategies for Mental Wellbeing

Adolescents with adjustment disorder benefit from proactive mental well-being interventions that take a comprehensive approach to supporting their emotional and psychological health. These tactics try to minimize or reduce the effect of stressors, identify indicators of adjustment issues, and promote resilience.

Education and awareness:

Increase awareness of adjustment issues among adolescents, caregivers, and educators. Understanding the signs and symptoms promotes early detection and intervention.

Promoting open communication:

Create an atmosphere in which teenagers feel free to communicate their feelings and difficulties. Encourage open communication with caregivers, instructors, and classmates to build a supporting network.

Building Resilience:

Implement programs or activities that encourage resilience, such as mindfulness, stress management, and skill-building exercises. Resilient teenagers are better prepared to face life's obstacles.

Healthy lifestyle choices:

Encourage healthy behaviors such as frequent exercise, a balanced diet, and enough sleep. Physical well-being promotes emotional resiliency and general mental health.

Peer Support Programs:

Establish peer support programs in schools or communities. Positive peer interactions provide teenagers with a feeling of belonging and may act as a helpful support network.

Counseling Services at Schools:

Integrate counseling services into educational settings to ensure that adolescents have easy access to assistance. School counselors may provide advice, coping skills, and a secure environment for addressing problems.

Mindfulness and relaxation techniques:
Teach mindfulness and relaxation strategies to teenagers so they may handle stress and concentrate better. These activities may include deep breathing techniques, meditation, or yoga.

Time Management Skills:
Provide resources and training for efficient time management. Helping teenagers arrange their duties might help them feel less overwhelmed and deal better with stress.

Parental Engagement and Support:
Encourage parents to assist their teens' mental health. Workshops, resources, and frequent contact may help parents understand and solve their children's specific issues.

Anti-bullying Initiatives:
Implement anti-bullying initiatives to foster a safe and inclusive atmosphere. Bullying may exacerbate adjustment issues, and preventative actions can assist preserve a pleasant school and social environment.

Life Skill Training:
Give teenagers vital life skills including problem solving, decision-making, and effective communication. These abilities help them handle problems and make good decisions.

Routine Check-Ins:
Set up regular check-ins with teenagers to measure their well-being. Regular examinations assist detect early indicators of adjustment issues and allow for prompt intervention.

Strengthening Coping Mechanisms

Strengthening coping mechanisms in adolescents with adjustment disorder entails providing them with appropriate stress management skills, problem-solving techniques, and resilience building. Recognizing symptoms of adjustment issues is critical for adapting coping techniques to meet individual requirements. Here's a thorough examination of ways to improve coping mechanisms:

Identification of stressors:
Begin by determining which particular stresses are contributing to the adjustment issue. Understanding the core reasons allows for the creation of focused coping techniques.

Psychoeducation:
Adolescents should be educated about adjustment issues, which will normalize the experience and reduce stigma. Knowledge enables people to detect symptoms early and seek help.

Cognitive Behavioral Therapy (CBT):
Cognitive behavioral therapy is an evidence-based treatment technique that assists teenagers in identifying and changing problematic thinking habits. It teaches kids coping skills and problem-solving solutions.

Mindful Practices:
Introduce mindfulness practices, such as meditation and mindful breathing, to assist teens in being present and managing overwhelming emotions. Mindfulness promotes self-awareness and emotional control.

Expressive Arts Therapy:

Involve teenagers in expressive arts treatments, such as painting or music therapy. Creative activities provide a nonverbal form of expression and may be used as a therapeutic coping method.

Journaling:

Encourage teenagers to maintain a notebook in which they may express their ideas and feelings. Journaling encourages self-reflection and may be a useful tool for processing tough events.

Social Support Networks:

Enhance social connections by cultivating supportive relationships with friends, family, and colleagues. Social support protects against stress and boosts resilience.

Problem-solving Skills:

Teach teenagers effective problem-solving techniques. Empowering individuals to examine problems, break them down into manageable chunks, and devise practical solutions improves their capacity to deal with pressures.

Relaxation techniques:

Deep breathing exercises, gradual muscular relaxation, and guided visualization may all be used to promote relaxation. These strategies assist in relieving physical and mental stress.

Positive self-talk:

Encourage positive affirmations and challenge negative self-talk. Helping teenagers reframe their beliefs in a more positive way promotes a better mentality.

Goal Setting:

Encourage goal setting as a means of providing direction and drive. Achieving modest, realistic objectives promotes a feeling of success and perseverance.

Time Management Skills:

Help teens establish excellent time management skills. Organizing chores and priorities may help lessen feelings of overload and improve coping.

Encourage healthy lifestyle habits.

Promote healthy behaviors such as frequent exercise, balanced eating, and enough sleep.

Physical well-being is intimately related to emotional resiliency.

Self-care Practices:
Emphasize the value of self-care. Adolescents should learn to prioritize things that offer them happiness, relaxation, and a feeling of balance in their lives.

Therapeutic interventions:
Engage in personalized therapeutic approaches, such as group therapy or individual counseling. These programs provide a structured environment for learning and practicing coping techniques.

Chapter 10: Community Resources and Support Networks.

Accessing Mental Health Services.

Accessing mental health assistance via community resources and support networks is critical for dealing with teenage adjustment issues. Recognizing indicators and delivering appropriate assistance requires good navigation of available resources. Here is a comprehensive exploration:

Education Outreach:

Community resources may launch educational initiatives to promote awareness about teenagers' adjustment issues. This includes lectures, seminars, and instructional materials to teach parents, educators, and community members how to recognize symptoms and seek treatment.

School-based Mental Health Services:

Collaborate with schools to build or improve mental health services on-site. School counselors, psychologists, and social workers may all help identify and assist teenagers who are having difficulty adjusting.

Community Mental Health Clinics:
Access local mental health clinics that specialize in teenage mental health. These clinics often provide a variety of services, including examinations, counseling, and treatment.

Hotlines & Helpline:
Provide information on mental health hotlines or helplines that teenagers and caregivers may use to get instant treatment or advice. These services may provide a listening ear, crisis assistance, or recommendations to relevant resources.

Online Counseling Services:
Look into online counseling systems that provide remote mental health help. This is particularly useful for teens, who may prefer the ease and privacy of virtual therapy.

Community Support Groups:
Organize or promote support groups for teenagers and their caretakers. These groups provide an

opportunity to share experiences, get direction, and develop a feeling of community.

Pediatricians and Primary Care Doctors:
Encourage parents to communicate with their pediatrician or primary care provider. These healthcare professionals may do initial evaluations, refer patients to experts, and give information on how to get mental health treatments.

Family Resource Centers:
Collaborate with family resource centers that provide a variety of services such as parenting courses, support groups, and referrals to mental health experts. These facilities may serve as useful hubs for comprehensive help.

Community Workshops and Training:
Organize seminars and training sessions for community members, such as teachers, clergy, and youth workers, to help them better understand adjustment problems and accessible support services.

Community-Based Organizations:
Connect with community-based groups dedicated to mental health advocacy and support. These organizations may provide services, financing, or programs geared toward teenagers and their families.

Crisis Intervention Services:
Ensure that community members have access to crisis intervention services. Having a clear strategy for dealing with mental health emergencies, including contact information for crisis intervention teams, is critical.

Insurance Navigation Assistance:
Offer information or support in determining insurance coverage for mental health care. Understanding insurance choices and coverage may make professional aid more accessible for families.

School-Based Prevention Programs:
Implement preventative programs in schools that focus on stress management, coping skills, and mental health awareness. Proactive measures may help to reduce the prevalence of adjustment problems.

Collaboration With Local Agencies:
Collaborate with local mental health organizations to establish a comprehensive network of services. Coordinated efforts guarantee that adolescents get complete and integrated care.

Community Events and Campaigns:
Participate in community activities and awareness efforts to help lessen stigma around mental health concerns. Normalizing interactions may allow teenagers and their families to seek treatment without fear of being judged.

Creating a Supportive Community for Adolescents

Building a supportive community for teenagers within community resources and support networks entails developing an atmosphere that promotes understanding, empathy, and accessibility in order to manage adjustment issues. Recognizing indicators and giving assistance requires a comprehensive strategy including a variety of community stakeholders. Here is a comprehensive exploration:

Educational and Awareness Programs:
Launch educational initiatives to promote awareness of adjustment problems among community members, such as parents, educators, and local leaders. These programs may include workshops, seminars, and educational resources.

School-based initiatives:
Collaborate with schools to create programs that provide a welcoming atmosphere. This might include anti-bullying campaigns, mental health awareness weeks, and promoting healthy peer connections.

Parental involvement:
Encourage parents to actively participate in their communities. Workshops, support groups, and parenting courses may all give resources and tools for detecting indicators of adjustment issues in teenagers.

Youth Engagement Programs:
Create youth engagement activities that give teenagers a safe area to express themselves and make relationships. These programs may include art

organizations, sports teams, or community service initiatives.

Mental Health Awareness Campaigns:

Launch mental health awareness initiatives to reduce the stigma associated with getting treatment for mental health disorders. This may include community events, social media campaigns, and collaborations with local media.

Community centers:

Establish or improve community centers that provide services and activities for teenagers. These facilities may provide counseling services, support groups, and recreational activities.

Peer Support Networks:

Facilitate peer support networks in schools and communities. Positive peer interactions may help provide emotional support and alleviate feelings of loneliness.

Mentoring Programs:

Create mentoring programs that link teenagers with good role models in their communities. Mentors provide direction, support, and a feeling of belonging.

Crisis Intervention Teams:
Teach crisis intervention skills to community people, such as teachers, leaders, and first responders. This guarantees that there are people available to give rapid assistance during times of need.

Collaboration With Local Businesses:
Engage local businesses to promote mental health programs. This might include sponsoring events, offering materials, or creating opportunities for teens to learn new skills and find jobs.

Religious and Spiritual Support:
Collaborate with religious or spiritual organizations to provide help to teenagers. These organizations may provide counseling services, community activities, and a feeling of belonging to persons seeking spiritual assistance.

Accessibility of Mental Health Services:
Advocate for better access to mental health services in the community. This might include collaborating with healthcare providers, insurance companies, and

local governments to ensure appropriate resources are accessible.

Community-Based Organizations:
Support and work with community-based groups that promote youth development and mental health. These organizations often provide essential resources and experience in meeting the specific needs of teenagers.

Creating Inclusionary Spaces:
Create an inclusive environment that values diversity and recognizes the specific issues that diverse groups of teenagers confront. This involves taking into account cultural, LGBTQ+, and other aspects that may contribute to adjustment challenges.

Regular Community Events:
Organize frequent community activities to bring people together. Building a feeling of community via events like fairs, festivals, and neighborhood meetings may help to establish social bonds and support networks.

CONCLUSION

In conclusion, managing adjustment problems in teenagers requires a comprehensive and coordinated effort that includes raising awareness, recognizing warning signals, and establishing strong support networks. The focus on adjustment disorder in teenagers highlights the necessity of early detection and intervention to enhance mental health. Here is a full analysis of the conclusion:

Importance of Early Recognition:
Emphasize the importance of identifying indicators of adjustment issues early on. Early detection enables early intervention and reduces the progression of mental health issues in teenagers.

Reducing Stigma:
Highlight the importance of reducing the stigma associated with mental health disorders, especially among teenagers. Creating a welcoming and inclusive atmosphere enables people to seek assistance without fear of being judged.

Collaboration among stakeholders:
Recognize the value of cooperation among diverse stakeholders, such as parents, educators, healthcare professionals, and community members. A collaborative effort guarantees a comprehensive approach to treating adjustment issues in teenagers.

Building Awareness:
Highlight the continued importance of community awareness campaigns and educational activities. Increasing understanding of adjustment disorders leads to a more educated and sympathetic society.

Empowering caregivers:
Recognize the importance of caregivers in the support network. Empowering parents and educators with tools, knowledge, and coping methods enables them to take an active role in teenagers' mental health.

Accessible Mental Health Services:
Advocate for better access to mental health treatments for teenagers in local areas. This involves increasing the availability of counseling, therapy, and crisis intervention services.

Community-Based Support:
Reinforce the significance of community-based support networks. Building a community that values mental health provides a safety net for teenagers, instilling a feeling of belonging and support.

Proactive Strategy:
Highlight the efficacy of proactive interventions including resilience-building activities, coping skill development, and stress management programs. These measures help in the prevention and early management of adjustment problems.

Family-Centered Approaches:
Highlight the efficacy of family-centered methods in the healing process. Engaging families in the treatment plan and offering support dramatically improves teenagers' overall well-being.

Strength-Based Approach:
Encourage a strengths-based approach to adjustment issues. Recognizing and building on teenagers' talents promotes a positive and powerful attitude toward their mental health journey.

Continued Collaboration:

Stress the need for ongoing cooperation among educational institutions, healthcare providers, and community groups. Ongoing relationships enable a consistent effort to assist adolescents encountering adjustment issues.

Crisis Preparation:

Recognize the significance of crisis preparation in communities. Having procedures in place to deal with mental health emergencies is critical for teenagers' safety and well-being.

Celebrate Diversity and Inclusion:

Accept the variety of teenagers and recognize the specific issues that each group faces. Creating inclusive places ensures that support systems are adapted to the community's different requirements.

Empowering adolescents:

Finally, emphasizes the need to provide teenagers with the skills, tools, and support networks they will need to navigate their mental health journey. Encouraging teenagers to take an active role in their own well-being promotes a feeling of agency and resilience.

In conclusion, the focus on adjustment disorder in teenagers necessitates a concerted and continuous effort to identify symptoms, offer prompt help, and provide an atmosphere that values mental well-being. We can help adolescents with adjustment issues improve their overall health and resilience by raising awareness, decreasing stigma, and developing strong community support networks.